Poems Reflections
The Black Experience

By

Andrew Lunn Sr

This book is a work of fiction. Places, events, and situations in this story are purely fictional. Any resemblance to actual persons, living or dead, is coincidental.

ISBN: 1-4033-6929-1 (e-book)
ISBN: 1-4033-6930-5 (Paperback)

Library Congress Control Number: 2002094115

This book is printed on acid free paper.

1stBooks - rev. 09/27/02

CONTENTS

iv

TERRORISM IN AMERICA

It was a bright summer day on eleventh of September,
A day all Americans and the world will remember.
A day when tragedy visited our shores,
The country called the melting pot with open arms and doors.
Terrorists struck with unimaginable devastation,
A blow so incredible as to paralyze a nation.
As the dark clouds of dust and smoke began to rise,
The lady on liberty island had tears in her eyes.
A sight too dreadful for innocent eyes to see,
Unbelievable destruction in the land of the free.
America and the world are still in mourning,
Trying to process this evil that had no warning.
Those cowardly terrorists could not foresee,
The resilience of average Americans like you and me.
Even with the obvious overwhelming grief,
Volunteers and rescue teams work without relief.
The sky line of our great nation is temporarily altered,
But make no mistake the American people will not falter.
If any good could come out of this dreadful act,
It is the strength of our resolve and that is a fact.

1

As personal stories of hardships still unfold,
We pray for the dead and deliverance of their souls.
Flags fly at half mast all over this great land,
Instilling patriotism in every child, woman, and man.
Just as certain as we can hear the ringing of our liberty bell,
We will follow and destroy those terrorists even into the jaws of hell.

ANCESTRAL SPIRIT CONNECTION

I looked in the mirror and I could see,
A shadowy figure hovering over me.
Startled, I turned myself around,
I saw nothing, then came a sound.
Be not afraid, it is only me,
The Nubian warrior from across the sea.
I am a spirit from another time and place,
I bring you a message from a people of grace.
Oh spirit from across the sea,
Why do want to connect with me?
You're the long lost child,
Your father reigns as king of the Nile.
I've traveled over time to watch and guide you,
From a distance, I've often sent you a clue.
Now, it is no longer a mystery,
You have become aware of your history.
I shall return to the land of the Nile,
To let your father know you're no longer a child.
There are many things you still do not know,
I've had the pleasure to watch you develop and
grow.
You are a proud Black man who has made a
valiant stand,
You are no longer a lost child in this far away
strange land.

THE DAY I SAW AN ANGEL

As a pre-teen when you came into my world,
I could see an angel inside a little girl.
I knew on that balmy spring day,
My life would change in every way.
I watched you from a distance, then got the nerve to speak,
The smile that came upon your face was such a delightful treat.
As time grew on when we became as one,
I was the earth and you were my morning sun.
We were inseparable for a love that was meant to be,
A story of love and friendship that is older than the sea.
As our family grew, I certainly knew that the lord had blessed us so,
He had placed an angel in our mist, what a precious gift to bestow.
When life dealt us a curve or two,
Your calmness and faith would pull us through.
Then came your declining health which you faced with such strength and courage.
As you laid on your dying bed, a light began to glow above your head.
You drifted into a deep,deep sleep,
I could see your wings sprouting right through the sheets.

I knew at that moment without a doubt,
God was reclaiming his angel he had only
loaned out.

ANGER

Brothers and sisters all over this land,
Angry at one another, angry at the man.
Caught up in a system of neglect and exploitation,
Feeling alienated from the rest of the nation.
Angry because neighborhoods have fallen into disrepair,
Angry because some politicians don't seem to care.
Angry because of stigmas that are attached to you,
Angry because others don't really have a clue.
Angry because the upwardly mobile have moved beyond your reach,
Angry because social ills don't allow teachers to teach.
Angry because safety has escaped your community,
Angry because you see there is very little unity.
Angry because violence has saturated your streets,
Angry because of all the young bodies covered by sheets.
Well! You have reasons to be angry but don't be misled,
Uncontrolled anger leaves too many of us dead.
Anger is like a cancer eating away at your soul,

Spreading through the community affecting the young and the old.
Harness that anger and listen to this appeal,
We must work together and take time to heal.
We must renew the spirit that gave our ancestors hope,
Let us trust one another and find new ways to cope.

PENNSYLVANIA AVENUE, THE GLORY DAYS

Step back into time on Pennsylvania Avenue,
Show place of the Black community I once knew.
It was a time when stage shows ruled the land,
Jazz musicians and entertainers backed by five piece bands.
Pennsylvania Avenue headlined in its hay day,
The likes of Count Basie and Cab Callaway.
Regulars like Moms Mabley, Red Foxx and Pig meat Marcum,
Doing his "Here Comes the Judge" that really sparked "um".
Standing in line at the Royal Theater for the famous midnight show,
That festive atmosphere of the avenue made it the place to go.
Ladies decked out in their party dresses with their fancy hairdos,
Men in their doubled breasted suits, wide brim hats and pointed toe shoes.
During a night out on the town,
The avenue was the place to hear the sounds.
Hitting club Casino, Comedy club and the York bar,
One could see all the stars without going to far.

This was a time when folks did not have a lot of money,
But for a reasonable sum it was a good place to impress your honey.
At night the avenue lit up like a Christmas tree all full of life,
With cheers and happy people dancing through the night.
You could step out of a club with your date for a short walk,
Always meeting a friend or someone who just wanted to talk.
Too bad the young folks don't share the memories of the avenue we knew,
But there are probably some older ones to that don't have a clue.
Don't you fret because it ain't over yet.
There are plans in the making to get the avenue back to moving and shaking.

BLACK MAN

Black Man! Oh Black Man!
How long shall ye slumber.
Brought in chains from Africa,
To a fate unknown in the West.
Auctioned from the blocks of Annapolis,,
Confused, weak and in need of rest.
Like a beast of burden, worked from sunrise to
sunset.
Beaten down even when you gave your best.
Black Man! Oh Black Man!
How long shall ye slumber.
Served in all major wars of the land,
Suffered every indignity at hand.
Rode in the Ninth and Tenth Cavalry,
Until your backside was raw.
Suffer you did still under the "Jim Crow" law.
Sweet land of liberty, yet you still strive to be
free.
Black Man! Oh Black Man!
How long shall ye slumber.
Remember our mighty warriors, like Douglas,
Malcolm and Martin.
With such great souls as these,
We should not become disheartened.
Remember our heroes, as we sat upon their
knees,
When they shared with us what it meant to be
free.

As bad as things seem today,
We still have Jessie Jackson and Kweisi Mfume.
Black Man! Oh Black Man!
How long shall ye slumber.
The Million Man March,what a sight to see,
One million plus Black brothers assembled in unity.
The progress we make in these uncertain times,
Can be wiped out with one quick headline.
Brothers killing brothers for no rhyme or reason,
Since the introduction of "Crack" it has been open season.
Senseless killings all over the land,
This could not be a part of the Master's plan.
As we approach the Millennium in our quest to be free,
I ask you my brother, who is the enemy?
Is it You? Or is it Me?

BLACK WOMAN

Black, majestic and queen of the Nile,
She's charming, beautiful, with an enduring
smile.

In more ways than one, she is like mother earth,
Black, fertile, and the giver of birth.

She moves gracefully to the rhythm of the
bongo,
Her roots lie deep in the middle of the Congo.

To be loved by her is nothing less than great,
She is the original woman others emulate.

Her emotions run deep down to her soul,
As she opens up, the mysteries unfold.

One is drawn to her like a bee to honey,
To possess her love is worth more than money.

On a scale from one to ten, she is an eleven,
Like an angel of God, she was sent here from
heaven.

Although she has suffered much pain
throughout the world,
It has not tarnished her image, for she remains a
black pearl.

Even though she is gentle and sensitive to touch,
She remains steadfast and comes through in a
clutch.

In matters that affect the ones she loves,
She displays the ferocity of a lioness protecting
her cubs.

She is a spiritual being who emits much love,
And credits her courage and strength to the
power above.

THE BLUES (A BLACK PERSPECTIVE)

From the time we stepped foot off the boat,
Cold weather caught us without a coat.
Had no choice but to forget your name,
Or feel the whip and endure the pain.
A pain that was felt inside your heart,
You knew that was the blues right from the start.
Worked all day and prayed all night,
To a God we had adopted to sustain us in this fight.
The blues is feeling the pain for your baby girl,
Whom you could not protect in this predatory world.
Lord have mercy on our souls,
Pressure like this, we can't expect to grow old.
The blues is not being able to show how you truly feel,
Being controlled and manipulated by one with eyes cold as steel.
Blues is being in this sweet land of liberty,
Knowing that your kind is a long ways from being free.
The blues is working a farm all day and into the night,
Still not having enough food to feed your family, that can't be right.

The Blues is living in this country from sea to shinning sea,
Not being able to travel fifty miles during a life time of misery.
The blues is living with stereotypes and be productive in our economy,
Only to be put down and face new obstacles, then told that you are lazy.
The Blues is living in the free world full of animosity,
Coping with all the prejudices and maintaining your sanity.
The fact that is unique about these black blues,
Is turning it into an art form that's been dubbed cool.
Blues is being able to sing and put to music the pain that you feel,
While telling the outside world of your experiences that are real.

JITTER BUG BLUES

"Hey Dey"! You with that silly smile,
Come! Talk to" yo homey" for awhile.
Ain't you got no problems at all,
Don't look like someone who just took a fall.
Man, I got problems up to my" ying yang"
Did two years for just being with the gang.
My old lady left me and the kids are uptight,
That boy of mine is just itching for a fight.
My daughter is walking the street and smoking
that crack,
I'm wearing this silly smile to keep those darn
tears back.
That's the truth of the matter and I ain't lying,
Man, I just laugh to keep from crying.
Still! I'm trying to get my life together,
Avoiding pitfalls and all that stormy weather.
Man! Life's dealt your boy one sorry hand,
Lay a ten spot on me...I'll pay you when I can.

MY FIRST CARNIVAL IN T&T

I met this sweet lady from T&T,
We went up to Brooklyn to meet her family.
It just happened to be the week of Labor Day,
Nothing could have prepared me for such a
wonderful stay.
Back yard parties were in full bloom'
Friendly "Trinis" winding to soca tunes.
Delicious food prepared by her folks,
My first taste of bust-up-shuts and curry goat.
The high light was the parade on Labor Day,
I saw the culture come alive on Eastern
Parkway.
This was my first experience of a real "Trini"
fete,
My lady looked at me and said," man yuh ain't
seen nutting yet".
If you want to see the real thing and the world's
greatest show,
I'll take you to the Caribbean islands of Trinidad
and Tobago.
Carnival fever was soon in the air,
We booked a flight and paid our fair.
We touched down at Piarco Airport,
Greeted by warm smiles and people in shorts.
Her sister met us at the airport whom we were
very happy to see,

She said we will rest a spell then visit our family.
From day one we traveled all over the land,
From open market places to the surf and the sand.
The first fete I experienced was at the Nestle's compound,
With sweet soca music and great bands all around.
Man this was one incredible sight,
The dancing and the music lasted into the night.
I was quite satisfied and worked up a big sweat,
My lady looked at me and said,'man yuh ain't seen nutting yet".
My next experience was the Soca Monarch Fiesta at Skinner Park,
That was some experience right from the start.
While trying to enter the park with our tickets in hand,
We suddenly felt the surge of very enthusiastic fans.
Stormers someone shouted and then out of the blue,
Came Policemen riding on horseback just as we got through.
I loved the excitement, but my lady was not very pleased,
The pushing and shoving brought some to their knees.
The show was fantastic and I had no regrets,

My lady looked at me and said,"man yuh ain't seen nutting yet".
My next great experience was at the Soca Village Fete,
Winding to"Crazy's" Nanny Wind left me all soak and wet.
Moving around the Country from North to South,
We stopped at every town without leaving one out.
The next big party was at a place called Fyzabad,
A place often visited by her brothers and her dad.
There was a sea of people and bands all around,
One of the biggest open air parties was found in this town.
I could not imagine what was to come after that great fete,
My lady still saying non-chalantly," yuh ain't seen nutting yet".
Our visit was into the second week with still a week to go,
My lady said you need this time to appreciate the world's greatest show.
By week's end I found myself in a place called the Big Yard. To get there calypsonians and musicians must work very hard.
The event was Panorama with at least 15 steel bands.

I was led by my lady's nephew up to the North Stand.
The stands were packed and excitement filled the air,
The crowd jumped and waved as if they had no cares.
By the time the last band crossed the stage, it was well into the night,
We continued to jump and wave until they were all out of sight.
I was so tired, all I wanted was a little sleep,
My lady and friends had to support me to help me stay on my feet.
We left Port Of Spain at the break of day,
Heading for South on Eastern Main Road and Solomon Ho-Choy Highway.
By the time we reach Cunupia, I had dozed off to sleep,
My lady nudged me to get back on my feet.
We went into the house to shower and eat,
Left a short time later and still no sleep.
I grabbed a carrib and a shot of Vat Rum,
While listening to the vibes of that magnificent steel drum.
Still heading South, we made a few stops on the way,
I could remember some one saying we have reached Debe.
My lady said let's get some doubles and more things to eat,

She turned to me and said try one you will enjoy this little treat.
I hesitated at first, then began to eat what turned out to be a hell of a treat.
We got back in the car still heading south to a town called Sipiria.
This is where my lady and her family is from,
We were going there to party and drink some good rum.
Met up with more friends and the rest of her folks,
Then headed for a beach party at a place called Los Iros.
We spent the rest of the day eating and dancing to that great soca beat,
Every one walking barefoot in the sand and me fighting the fire ants eating at my feet.
I went for a swim in sea, came out soaking wet,
My lady still dancing and smiling said "Man yuh ain't seen nutting yet".
With Carnival winding down my lady said there are still a few things to go,
We purchased tickets to the great event called the Demarche Gras show.
This was one spectacular event, with calypsonians coming from all the tents.
Back to Port Of Spain we now reach, As the calypsonians come out to do two tunes each.
This was also the event for the competition for king and queen of carnival.
Costumes like nothing I had ever seen before,

Such magnificent designs winding across the floor.
I know this had to be all there was to see,
My lady smiled and said come follow me.
We spent the night in town at her friend's home in Woodbrook,
A warm friendly lady and such a good cook.
We had another carib each and then had to pass,
At the break of dawn, we were off to something called Mud "Mas".
This was an exciting parade to see,
People covered with mud from there head to there feet.
This was followed by the parade of bands,
Thousands wearing colorful costumes and waving their hands.
This was indeed a wonderful experience and now it is time to go,
I looked at my lady and said this is the world's greatest show.

CARIBBEAN WOMAN

Moving from Island to Island under the hot Caribbean sun,
There lies a most delectable flower in this land of surf and fun.
From spice Island to the land of calypso,
Catch a glimpse of this flower's special glow.
From downtown Bay street during festive junkanoo,
To the streets of Port of Spain's carnival rhythm of the tamboo.
This beautiful flower comes in all races and creeds,
She has the graceful movements that will bring men to their knees.
She is hot like pepper and sweet as a julie mango,
She brings joy to all in the land of the shango.
Caribbean Woman who speaks with an accent sure to please,
When vexed her tongue will lash out with the greatest of ease.
She has many wonderful qualities and loves to tease,
Can be cunning and devilish under a warm summer breeze.
She dances to soca music and the cool vibes of reggae,

Nothing comes close to her when she's out to play.
There is no other flower that can match her for beauty and fun,
She is nourished and cultivated under the warm Caribbean sun.

CONSPIRACY

(WORD ON THE STREET)

A brother on the street said to me,
I hear some talk about a conspiracy.
They said the "Gov'ment" brought in drugs,
Talk like that must be coming from thugs.
I just heard the other day,
Some congressman said it was the CIA
Angry lawmakers calling for an investigation,
While drugs keep flowing through Penn Station.
Talk like that got people uptight
Began to blame the "Gov'ment" for our plight.
Fool!, our "Gov'ment" want us to be free,
All you have to do is check out your history.
Some say the "Gov'ment" holding its head in
the sand,
Meanwhile "Crack" has infiltrated the land.
This "Gov'ment" that seems to work so well,
Surely wouldn't contribute to that road to hell.
Well!, let's take a little look see,
Policy like that affects you and me.
What the "Gov'ment" going do with the
brothers on the street,
Word is they rather get high than find
something to eat.
They have on their hands plenty of time,
Will take your life for a nickel or a dime.

Jails filled to capacity with young African brothers,
Bringing plenty of despair to their overworked mothers.
Damn! This talk about a conspiracy,
Beginning to make more sense to me.
Remember those Black men down in Tuskegee?
Folks say the"Gov'ment" was behind that catastrophe.
Many enlightened brothers calling for unity,
Some swear the "Gov'ment" trying to destroy our community.
Fool! The "Gov'ment" is going to give us a hand,
Yeah! The same "Gov'ment" that called us three-fifths of a man.
WOW! "Gov'ment" having thoughts like that makes it easy to see,
Why a brother would think there is a conspiracy.
Wake up Black people! The handwriting is on the wall,
Show young Black brothers how to walk tall!
Teach them responsibility and let's reverse this trend,
Give them knowledge to enable them to be proud Black men.

CRY BABY

From infancy we learn to cry,
Mothers seem to know the reason why.
Unable to speak a word to mention,
We often cry to get attention.
As we grow, develop and stand on our feet,
We stop crying and begin to speak.
As a child, responsibilities we had just a few,
Getting an education was one we had to do.
To prepare for the world of work is really quite
hard,
Can not be accomplished spending idle time in
the yard.
To have a chance, one must develop a good skill,
Important ingredients include patience and a
strong will.
Still, the good life is not automatic,
It is filled with setbacks and plenty of static.
So stop crying!! No time to whine!!
Pick up the pieces! Leave negative thoughts
behind.
For those who think doing drugs is really very
cool,
You are floating in space and playing the fool.
There has never been a level playing field,
Hard work, determination and focus are the real
deal.
No time to quit and throw in the towel,
No time to cry and holler foul.

Our forefathers faced life with so much less,
We certainly must try to give it our best.
We must continue to go forward even under
stress,
When we accomplish our goals we can take time
to rest.
Strive for perfection and reach for the sky,
No one will listen if you continue to cry.
Wipe away those tears! Face up to your fears!
Stand tall and you will see! You can control your
destiny.

FALSE HOPE

What started out as a trip for fun,
Proved to be costlier than one holding a gun.
Greeted by flashing lights and the ringing of
bells,
Stares on people faces and cigarette smells.
The sound of slots ringing had filled the air,
People rushing to and fro without any care.
Some standing and waiting for their favorite
machines,
Others claiming two and looking real mean.
Ladies stepping out dressed in their Sunday
best,
While others are depressed and looking a mess.
Bells constantly clanging in what seems to be
fun,
The truth of the matter is that very few had won.
Finally, you get a machine of your choice,
With spectators standing over you and loosing
their voice.
You sit there for hours while a few coins fall,
Feeding that darn machine and ignoring
nature's call.
Sooner or later you figure to hit a small jackpot,
Only to be wiped out by those insatiable slots.
You search your pockets frantically with no
money to be found,
Off you go to find an ATM with the accuracy of
a bloodhound.

You return to your machine with hopes that you will win,
But you see the same cycle repeat over and over again.
Sitting there dejected, looking like you lost your best friend,
You remember the looks on people's faces when you came in.
Passing all the losers on your way out,
You began to hear the message the P A system shouts.
If you think you have a problem you can't handle,
Get help by calling 1-800 Gambler.

FATHERS IN THE HOOD

Peace my brother...Shalom...Asalama lei kum,
Hats off to true fathers throughout the Nation.
Will the real fathers please stand up,
Not you who burry your sorrows in a cup.
Hats off to fathers that sometimes fall,
But find the strength and courage to answer the call.
Hats off to fathers that teach their children to pray,
Who assists with spiritual development instead of running away.
Hats off to the fathers who keep their family together,
Not pointing the finger of blame when besieged by stormy weather.
Hats off to those fathers that don't impose their will,
And become abusive when they've truly had their fill.
Hats off to those fathers that don't spend their leisure time on the street,
But spend quality time nurturing their children...wow! That's neat.
Hats off to those fathers who have not fallen from grace,
When they approach their love ones, you see a smile come to their face.

Andrew Lunn Sr.

Hats off to the fathers that remain fathers until the end,
By being a part of their family's life the entire community wins.

FISH SANDWICH& A BOTTLE OF BEER

Last summer I visited my cousin in a small
country town,
I drove around for miles and miles and not one
night club could be found.
At the end of a week, I was ready to leave,
Then my cousin said I know a little joint that's
sure to please.
We jumped in my ride and headed for the next
town,
Passed through some woods then began to hear
the sounds.
Music came blasting right off the tree sounding
like an old time jamboree.
Made our way through the trees that led to a
small door,
Saw a good number of patrons shaking the old
dance floor.
Red, green and yellow lights flashing,
People singing and dancing like it was going out
of fashion.
Up on the stage was a four piece band,
And a gorgeous babe with a mike in her hand.
She poured out tunes with such delight,
Man! I could listen to this chick for the rest of
the night.
While" cuz "joined the people on the dance floor,
I asked that fox to sing some more.

She noticed me sitting there with that big silly grin,
She had finished her last tune then started over again.
At her break, the fellows buzzed around her like she was a queen bee,
Her eyes met mine and she decided to sit with me.
"Hey baby" she said "Are you having a good time",
Yes, I replied, I'm doing just fine.
I complimented her on her singing and asked that she have a drink with me,
We sat there engaged in deep conversation until half past three.
Wow! She said Time certainly flies,
At that moment, she caught me looking at her thighs.
Hey baby, you like what you see,
Yes, I said as she pulled her skirt above her knee.
She smiled and moved closer to my side,
Then whispered in my ear baby I'm going to need a ride.
I asked if there is anything you need my dear,
Then she said softly a fish sandwich and a bottle of beer.
We jumped in the car and up the road we went,
We came to a small cabin right next to a tent.
She smiled at me showing those big pearly whites,

Baby I hope you're prepared to stay all night.
When I woke up, I could see her body was real
fine.
Arms and legs all wrapped around mine.
I looked at her and I could still hear "fish
sandwich and bottle of beer.

DON'T GAMBLE WITH YOUR SOUL

I live a life plain and simple,
No exciting stories to be told.
I believe in peaceful coexistence,
And the hopes of one day growing old.
I believe in hard work and fair play,
When things are going smooth, sometimes I
forget to pray.
I often take for granted all the good that
happens to me,
Forgetting that all is made possible by the man
from Galilee.
One day as I was relaxing, I felt a slight chill,
Followed by calmness, then a voice said "peace
be still".
I was feeling safe and comfortable as a believer
of the word,
Until that moment of awakening from the
message that I heard.
If you want to receive the crown of life don't
pursue riches and gold,
But be ye doers of the word and don't gamble
with your soul.
After this revelation, it is plain for me to see,
To enter his kingdom and have eternal life
follow the one from Galilee.
From out of darkness and into the light no
mystery to behold,

Accept your new birth as God's true servant and don't gamble with your soul.

A HOSTILE ENVIRONMENT

Listen young brothers and you will see,
How you can refuse to be one out of three.
Negative statistics all over the land,
Primary focus is of course the Black man.
The system has already decided your destiny,
By telling the world you're one out of three.
One-third of young Black men in jail, on probation or parole,
This is how that story unfolds.
From grade school you're branded as one who can't follow the rule,
You are dealt with improperly and soon labeled a fool.
With pent up emotions and no place to turn,
Without hesitation you're told you can't learn.
Soon lost in the system like a minnow in the ocean,
Year after year you receive a social promotion.
Leaving high school still desperately in need,
Comes the realization you're unable to read.
Jobs that are available require a higher skill,
When told you're not qualified it becomes a bitter pill.
You start to doubt yourself because of the negative things you're heard,
The self fulfilling prophecy comes true to the last word.

Lost and bewildered with some of your youth
spent,
You take a good look around and find you're in
a hostile environment.
For some who excel in sports, you are given a
slight reprieve,
You are embraced by the larger society and
become objects of their greed.
But if you step out of line you too will soon see,
Just like many others you face the same destiny.
So listen up young brothers, don't let the system
determine your fate.
Find positive role models that you can emulate.
Improve your image and learn to love yourself,
Pool your resources and begin to enjoy the
wealth.
Love thee one another, show respect towards
your brother.
Break the cycle of violence, and let go of that
mentality,
That gives you the dubious distinction of being
one out three.

JOURNEY INTO HELL

They came during the day,
They came during the night.
They burned and plundered everything in sight.
Destroying entire villages and people at will,
Those they could not subdue they would surely
kill.
Bound and gagged and kept under restraint,
Men, women and children marched until they'd
faint.
Some were very weak and became sick on the
way,
Whipped until they dropped, would not see the
light of day.
Marched towards the coast without explanation,
Their destination ahead, the Goree Island
station.
Scrutinized, sized and sorted like cattle,
Some used and abused since the initial battle.
Chained to walls in dungeon like cells,
Being kept awake by horrible screams and yells.
Watching and waiting with very much concern,
Finally, marched through the doorway where no
one returns.
Taken to a slave ship somewhere off shore,
Packed in like sardines down under the floor.
What lies ahead is too horrible to tell,
This was the beginning of the journey into hell.

LEGACY OF LOVE

We gather today to celebrate,
The life and impact of a mother's love.
Deeply rooted in God's love,
Delivered to us by one known as"Moah".
Her message was the same for family as well as
strangers,
Love never fails even in the face of danger.
To know her was to love her,
This fact was plain to see.
We must keep her dream alive,
And continue her legacy.
As we count our blessings and cherish the fond
memories,
We thank God for blessing her with all these
wonderful seeds.
Thinking now with gratitude of all her good
advice,
All of her guidance through the years and all of
her sacrifice.
Time will not dim the the kindness of her deeds,
Her ministry to her family and others who were
in need.
To honor her we must be faithful in our walk
with the lord,
Loving and protecting one another without any
discord.

As we celebrate her life and the simple things
she taught you and me,
We discover it was what was in her heart that
proved to be the key.
Yes! Her's truly was a legacy of love,
What a precious gift to give by this lady known
as "Moah".

LYNCHING

I close my eyes and I still see,
A vision of my country on a lynching spree.
Men, women, and children all came forth,
Ready to take part in this spectator sport.
The look on some faces filled with glee,
A disturbing view from a large poplar tree.
Slavery had been abolished in the land of the free,
But soon to be replaced by a lynching spree.
At times it would happen without explanation,
A terrible blight on a very promising nation.
Many of those lynched were in local custody,
Supposedly protected by the authority.
Crowds with pack mentality of the wild,
Broke into jails not permitting a trial.
Faced with trumped up charges and nothing concrete,
People were humiliated and dragged through the street.
Bodies beaten and bludgeoned from their head to their feet.
Some were dipped in oil and burned alive,
One could hear their horrible screams and awful cries.

As shameful as these acts may be, they must be uncovered for all to see.

America has to face its horrible past for healing process to begin at last.

THE MELTING POT

America is a blend of more than one community,
People coming together in a sense of unity.
Everyone working together throwing in their lot,
The country affectionately known as a melting pot.
Now a dark cloud has settled over the land,
What used to be our strength now divides the common man.
Different ethnic groups which have made this country great,
Have been targeted by extremists and become objects of their hate.
The pot is boiling over as tempers begin to rise,
The lady on Liberty Island has tears in her eyes.
Mean spirited politicians feed into this awful brew,
What's needed is trust and patience to calm down this stew.
Anti-terrorist laws that discourage immigration,
Is not the cure we need for that which ails the nation.
To make things right there is a way to start,
Begin the healing process by opening one's heart.
Problems we face as a country fallen from grace,

Andrew Lunn Sr.

Can only be solved by including every creed
and race.
The cultural diversity which has made this
country great,
Has to resurface before it becomes too late.
As we approach the millennium the test for us
will be,
To put our nation back on track to face a new
century.

MEMORIES OF LOVE

How precious this gift of Love,
From one so sweet, so soft, so dear.
To look upon your smiling face,
Was to see all that is good of this human race.
To walk and talk with you was such a delight,
To have shared your love is reason to continue
this fight.
You meant so much to so many people,
You touched so many lives with your kindness
and thoughtfulness.
All of these attributes were much greater than
having wealth,
They seemed to serve you well even in your
declining health.
As I think back,it's easy to remember,
The onset of your illness started in December.
The news was so devastating I could hardly
stand,
You showed such strength and courage as you
held out your hand.
As we cried out with emotion on that dreadful
day,
I prayed the lord would take me for you so
deserved to stay.
As fate would have it, we got a slight reprieve,
GOD granted us two more years knowing you
still must leave.

Andrew Lunn Sr.

It was so painful to see the love of my life fade
away,
Your faith remained so strong until your dying
day.
I will not dwell on sickness, the trials nor the
strife,
But the joy you brought to all because of your
precious life.

MOTHER

Praises and glory to the creator,
For the unselfish love of a mother.
It was not by accident but by design,
He gave to her qualities he gave no other.
One who appears like a beacon of light,
To comfort a frightened child awakened in the night.
One who rises in the morning before all others,
Preparing for her love ones asleep under the covers.
One who teaches us how to pray,
As we face the challenges of a another day.
One who helped us to face the rigors of school,
While constantly reminding us of the golden rule.
One who kept us in line and at times would certainly fuss,
She would never let us forget that in God we must trust.
After completing our chores with the house clean and neat,
She would always come through with a very special treat.
As we face life's struggles and the road uphill,
We think of her courage and her undying will.
We thank God for fathers, sisters and brothers,
But most of all we thank him for giving us mothers.

Andrew Lunn Sr.

MY LOVE OF MUSIC

Few things mean more to me,
Than the sound of sweet harmony.

Music, the art form whose media is sound,
Can arouse every emotion around.

To spend a relaxing day on the beach,
seems more rewarding with soft music in reach.

Music governs my entire day,
Whether it's at work or play.

There is nothing like a musical score,
Can put a baby to sleep or send men off to war.

Music can be felt deep in one's soul,
Enjoyed by the young as well as the old.

I like to listen to soca, calypso and reggae,
My personal favorite is jazz, be it night or day.

I play cassettes and albums until they are worn,
Love to listen to the melody of Dexter's sweet
horn.

Sweet tunes, there are more than just a few,
Some are very old and others brand new.

When I am in a mellow mood with nothing to
do,
I turn on some jazz and blues too.

Instrumentals and vocalists, they both have
much to say,
I like the smooth sound of Cannonball and the
vibes of Lady day.

I can't imagine what life without music would
be,
Personally, it would be like a Forrest without a
tree.

I will continue to enjoy music as I grow old,
The only way for me to stop is when I become
cold.

WALKING TO NOWHERE

The sun was shining on this pleasant and clear day,
A slight chill filled the air, it was the early part of May.
The sounds of the city started to come alive,
People walking by briskly, some taking long strides.
I had just left my comfortable home for the night,
Somewhere behind the dumpsters among the rats and blight.
My clothes are disheveled and I look out of place,
I try not to be noticed as I cover my face.
I am careful to blend in with the crowd with my belongings in tow,
I walk with direction as if I have someplace to go.
As I walk, I wonder why this could be happening to me,
I once had a pretty good life and worked for a good company.
The power lunches, booze and drugs contributed to my fall,
Not being able to manage the good life was when I dropped the ball.
So I walk and I walk as if I don't have a care,
I walk constantly but I am going nowhere.

SWEET TALK

This is a story of a smooth talking gigolo,
Who presented a pleasant smile wherever he'd go.
He was soft spoken and considered a lady's man,
Always willing to lend a helping hand.
He would promise to give you diamonds and pearls,
Had mature ladies acting like teenage girls.
He would make promises that were sure to please,
But deep within him it was only a big tease.
He would do little things that a lady would talk about,
With carefully picked sweet words coming from his mouth.
What was the ulterior motive of this very calculated man,
It was obviously well thought out, yet a very simple plan.
He played on ladies that were lonely and out of the loop, Bombard them with sweet talk until they were ripe to swoop.
He had prior commitments and baggage galore,
Always had a list of excuses when he entered the door.
Disappointments came one after the other,

One would think this would certainly blow his cover.

But when a lady is in love, she is the last to see,

What this gigolo has made so clear to you and me.

TIME

It's all about time!
All things are governed by time.
From the creation of earth,
To conception and birth.
From the cultivation of precious pearls,
To the proper development of boys and girls.
As infants we are placed on the clock to be fed,
Awake a short time then whisked off to bed.
A time for school and a time for play,
A time to collect our thoughts as we began a
new day.
We rush off to work running to and fro,
Only to be stuck on the expressway with no
place to go.
Tic Tock! Tic Tock! There is no stopping that
darn clock.
We break out of work like horses out of stalls,
To consume everything we can at those
shopping malls.
We arrive home at the end of the day,
With more work to be done and no time for
play.
This cycle repeats itself over and over,
Tic Tock! Tic Tock! No stopping that darn clock.
Then, one day as the cycle begins to stall,
We notice the clock has stopped on the wall.
Be it spring, summer, winter or fall,
The time has come to answer that final call.

Andrew Lunn Sr.

As we enter the spirit world there is no reversal,
We suddenly realize this was no dress rehearsal.
We look back over the course of time,
Too late to help your brother that asked for a dime.
While the clock is still ticking up on the wall,
Take the time to help someone before that final call.

LOSS TREASURES

As one travels through the schools it's plain to
see,
Some one has dropped the ball and that's no
mystery.
Our children are suffering and crying out for
help,
While displaying unimaginable behavior that is
certainly being felt.
Profane words that are spoken as if taught in a
special course,
Flow from students mouths with no feeling of
remorse.
Our teachers are bewildered and obviously
disgusted,
To witness the horrible attitudes of those they
are entrusted.
Parents hang their heads in shame,
Knowing they must share some blame.
Year after year our schools fail to make the
grade,
High goals for student achievement began to
fade.
The ills of society transcend our school walls,
It is quite obvious as one pass through the halls.
What is wrong with a system with funds and
special tools,
To find itself in utter chaos where few follow the
rules.

Andrew Lunn Sr.

What is this phenomenon called "Special Ed.",
Where five or six professionals try to get into the
student's head.
Students loss in the system like a minnow in the
ocean,
Year after year receiving a social promotion.
Leaving high school still desperately in need,
Many of our students still can not read.
What can we do and how can we measure,
All the simple things that once gave us pleasure.
Back to basics is easier said than done,
Persevere we must until this battle is won.
We must continue to strive for perfection in this
imperfect world,
In order to preserve the loss treasures, our
precious boys and girls.

IF TREES COULD TALK

I AM A TREE AND I GET NO RESPECT,
MY PURPOSE FOR BEING IS TO KEEP
NATURE IN CHECK.
ANCIENT MAN COULD NOT HAVE
TRAVELED THE SEA,
IF NOT FOR THE WOOD PROVIDED BY A
TREE.
I GIVE YOU SHELTER AND THE MEANS TO
KEEP YOU WARM,
PROVIDE YOU WITH HOMES TO COME IN
OUT OF THE STORM.
HOW AM I REPAID FOR ALL OF THESE
GREAT DEEDS,
BY SO MUCH UNDERBRUSH AND CHOKING
WEEDS.
YOUR PRECIOUS DOGS CAN'T PASS BY ME,
WITHOUT RAISING THEIR HIND LEGS TO
WET ME WITH PEE.
YOU CARVE ALL SORTS OF MESSAGES ON
ME,
AND THEN SAY SO WHAT, IT'S ONLY A
TREE.
THERE WAS A TIME WHEN YOU WOULD
HANG FLESH ORNAMENTS
ON ME,
AND DOUSE THEM WITH OIL FOR ALL
OTHERS TO SEE.

YOU SLAM YOUR VEHICLES INTO ME AS IF
I AM IN YOUR WAY,
I TELL YOU, IF I COULD TALK THESE ARE
THINGS THAT I 'D SAY.
I WONDER WHAT YOU WOULD DO IF I JUST
PICK UP AND LEAVE,
DO YOU NOT REALIZE WITHOUT ME YOU
COULD NOT BREATHE.
SO THE NEXT TIME YOU SEE A TREE,
THANK GOD HE CREATED ME.
TRIM MY BRANCHES AND PRUNE MY
LEAVES AND FOR GOODNESS
SAKE CURVE THAT DARN DOG WHO
WANTS TO PEE WHEN HE SEES
A TREE

TRIBUTE TO BIG BROTHER

It was in May around Mother's day,
when the Angel of Death took big brother away.
As I sat and watched with my eyes on the hearse,
I think of big brother in a series of firsts.
He was the first born, first to walk,
First to utter a word, first to talk.
First to face the challenges of life,
Filled with trials, tribulations and strife.
As a young man still in his teens,
He joined the Army wearing blue jeans.
Six months later after assignment to the 24th Infantry,
He was a prisoner of war who yearned to be free.
A letter from the Army and this is what it said,
Big brother is missing in action and presumed dead.
This! Mother believed not to be so,
If it were true surely God would let her know.
Months and years went by slowly, then the letters began to come.
The family gathered around as mother read them one by one.
Thirty months later, after living under tyranny,
Came the news that P.O.W.'s soon would be free.

Each evening we listened, as the prisoners were exchanged,
When finally the old Philco radio echoed his name.
We yelled and screamed and all began to shout,
We prayed for a moment, then pandemonium broke out.
After a period of time spent in Army hospitals abroad,
Came the day we all waited for, thanks to the Lord.
A celebration like nothing I would ever see,
People came from miles around to join a hero's block party.
Big brother was back to claim his rightful place,
As he looked at the small apartment, he said "mother we need more space".
His first order of business, with his kind and giving heart,
Was to see that mother and siblings get off to a brand new start.
With cash in hand, this giant of a man proceeded to look for a house,
A short time later his lord and savior delivered unto him a spouse.
As his family grew, he certainly knew the lord had blessed him so.
Like the time he shared a war story how God carried him through ice and snow.
There were times when he grew weary, with some periods of indecision.

TRIBUTE TO BIG BROTHER

He pressed on to do God's work because he had
a vision.
He labored hard and long, with devoted wife
and children by his side,
This giant of man would stop for nothing
including his foolish pride.
Finally, it all came together in spite of sickness
and poor health,
This valiant soldier had pursued his dream
which for him became his wealth.
He planted the seeds in his garden and stood by
to watch them grow,
When he heard the voice of a mighty God say
servant it's time to go.
It happened in May around Mother's Day, when
the Angel of Death took big brother away.
Through all the pain, sickness and strife, death is
a small
price to pay when the reward is eternal life.

ENEMY IN THE VILLAGE

Hey! Hey! Back in the day,
When there was unity in the community.
When block parties were an integral part of
community life,
Without drugs, violence and present day strife.
When sneaking into a movie theater was
considered a capital crime,
Caught by any adult neighbor who had the
authority to dust off your behind.
The extended family consisted of the entire
neighborhood,
In the absence of parents, this was very much
understood.
When teachers could discipline their students
and not worry about being sued,
Or much worst be violently attached right there
in the school.
It was a time when family values peaked,
Young people represented themselves well at
home as well as on the street.
Profane and inappropriate language was very
seldom heard,
To do so would certainly result in swift
punishment for those unspoken words.
Respect for self and others was very much
understood,
This was common among families throughout
the neighborhood.

We must examine our society that is in a state of social and moral decay,
That would force our children to turn to drugs just to get through another day.
The village is now under a state of seize with escalating crime and violence bringing it to its' knees.
We must rally the troops to face this enemy from within,
That has dishonored our women and slaughtered our men.
We must reclaim our neighborhoods block by block,
And restore the village to its' proper place while there is still time left on the clock.

Andrew Lunn Sr.

VIOLENCE

My wish is that I might live to see,
Violence disappear from our community.

It has taken over the land by storm,
Happens so often it has become the norm.

It happens when tempers flare,
It happens because some don't care.

To some it happens just by chance,
To others it could be over a silly glance.

It is in the home as well as on the street,
It can even happen while you are fast asleep.

It happens too often in the neighborhood store,
The owner's at risk as he opens his door.

It can happen whether it's night or day,
It happens to our children at school or play.

We must act now to reverse this trend,
Bring peace to our community again.

We can not sit by idle without a plan,
While we witness man's inhumanity to man.

To conquer this evil we must work and pray,

With God's help we shall see a brighter day.

WHO AM I

I am the super superman,
I do things no one else can.
I work long hours for little or no pay,
Up at the break of dawn each and every day.
I try to make myself invisible and stay out of sight,
Though I make the six o'clock news almost every night.
I play a big part in the prison growth industry in these United States,
Because I am incarcerated disproportionately at such an alarming rate.
Though life is rough and at times a living hell,
Through blood, sweat and tears, I continue to excel.
I am loyal to a system I have sworn to defend,
I go willingly where my government decides to send.
I play by the rules designed to keep things stable,
I have to make a fuss to get a seat at the table.
Constantly scrounging for crumbs and feeling much like mice,
I get fed up and angry and then told to be nice.
I am often called on without much relief,
To support a system that gives me nothing but grief.
But I can handle whatever the dish,

We are fast approaching the time when I'll get
my wish.
Who am I? According to the creator's plan,
I am not super, I am a black man.

UNDER THE WILLOW TREE

It was in May, no June you see,
As I sat beneath the old willow tree.
Gently swaying in the breeze,
I felt the softness of its leaves.
As I relaxed and enjoyed the pleasant smell,
Little did I know this area had a story to tell.
I dozed off to sleep with my head on the earth,
Feeling secure in the land of my father's birth.
Suddenly! A black cloud settled over the tree,
I thought I heard a scream, Mercy...! Mercy...!
As I Awoke and looked around,
I saw in the distance the source of the sound.
There! Stood a large Poplar tree,
Echoing the words...Mercy!...Mercy...!
I tried to stand but my legs were too weak,
I looked and listened but dare not speak.
I saw nothing but then heard the sound,
I knew with certainty there were spirits around.
As I focused on this sound of distress,
I sensed the spirit was yearning to rest.
I listened intensely and heard the spirit say,
Please! Please! Don't treat me this way.
After these words came a distressing yell...!
And shortly thereafter a very pungent smell.
It was the smell of burning flesh,
A story the tree yearned to confess.
Suddenly, it began to rain,
Slowly washing away the spirit's pain.

The black cloud drifted and the sun shone bright,
As if to signal the spirit to follow the light.
This message was revealed to me,
When I fell asleep under the old willow tree.

-PREFACE-

There have been many stories told of the plight of African slaves making the journey from their homeland and traveling to a world very foreign to them.

This is a story of five men who were captives that were bound together in chains and never made it through the middle passage. Faced with a language barrier, it shows how they developed means to communicate and form a bond under very stressful conditions and ever present dangers.

JOURNEY INTO HELL

They came during the day,
They came during the night.
They burned and plundered everything in sight.
Destroying entire villages and people at will,
Those they could not subdue they would surely
kill.
Bound and gagged and kept under restraint,
Men, women and children marched until they'd
faint.
Some were very weak and became sick on the
way,
Whipped until they dropped, would not see the
light of day.
Marched towards the coast without explanation,
Their destination ahead, the Goree Island
station.
Scrutinized, sized and sorted like cattle,
Some used and abused since the initial battle.
Chained to walls in dungeon like cells,
Being kept awake by horrible screams and yells.
Watching and waiting with very much concern,
Finally, marched through the doorway where no
one returns.
Taken to a slave ship somewhere off shore,
Packed in like sardines down under the floor.
What lies ahead is too horrible to tell,
This was the beginning of the journey into hell.

THE BONDING

Somewhere in the middle of the Atlantic Ocean in the eighteenth century a slave ship destined for the Americas carried a cargo of seventy-two slaves. Stolen from West Africa, the slaves came from many different tribes and villages. They feared for their lives and at best faced a very uncertain future. They did not understand the strange tongue of their captors and even more discouraging they could not understand the language of many of their African brothers who were also held in bondage. The conditions that they were forced to live under on this ship were horrific. The men and women were forced to relieve themselves where they were held under restraint.

Because there had been many uprisings and rebellions on slave ships, movement of the captives was limited. In spite of the tight security and horrible conditions encountered on the journey many slaves were still able to form bonds. This is a story of one such bonding. Five male slaves from different villages in Africa were chained together. None of them spoke the same dialect, which made communication almost impossible. Faced with this language barrier, they still had some things in common. They were all captives and were heading for an unknown fate. They had heard stories from their tribesmen of villagers being stolen or captured and never seen or heard from again. There worst fears were now being realized.

These five men, not able to speak each other's language as much as they tried had to find a way to communicate. Under heightened security, this task became even more difficult. The five men that were chained together were Amadou, Ibrahima, Akim, Abdullah, and Zumbulu. Each evening before the sunset the men were brought topside chained and shackled. They were made to exercise and were washed down by the sailors pulling buckets of water from the sea and tossing it on the men. The slaves began to communicate by signaling each other with the movement of their eyes and facial expressions.

One evening as they were going through this ritual, the five slaves saw a few of the crewmen carrying a captive that was very sick and near death tossed over board. The five men looked at each other and at that moment realized that this brother would suffer no more. Death had deprived the whites of their precious cargo. For the next week, the five captives communicated by using eye signals and facial expressions. They knew what they had to do in order to prevent themselves from being sold into a life of slavery. They watched and waited for the opportunity to carry out their plan. They all were thinking about the brother that was tossed overboard being freed from a life of servitude.

One evening when the five captives were on deck, they got the chance they were waiting for. Some of the young female slaves were brought on the deck to be washed down with the seawater. They were standing on deck naked and shivering while the crewman gazed upon their bodies making obscene comments to each other. While the crewmen were preoccupied lusting over the young black beauties, the five men chained together seized this opportunity to carry out their plan. Amadou leading the charge toward the ship's side let out with a fierce cry...Allah Akbar...God is great. He then threw his body overboard with the other four men following in tow. With none of the captives resisting, the weight of the first helped to pull the others who followed willingly. Within seconds, the five comrades were in the water with their bodies heading for the bottom of the sea.

FROM THE DEPTHS

The five slaves met a quick and certain death as their bodies reached the bottom of the sea. They thought they would accomplish this freedom in death. Soon they would realize that they were still very far from being free.

By committing suicide, they had sinned against God and would not enter his kingdom without undergoing a cleansing process. Even in the spirit world the five men were still bound together. There was one very interesting change that occurred as spirits; the five captives were now able to understand and speak to each other freely.

They discussed their situation between themselves and decided to ask God what could be done to prepare them to enter his kingdom. God answered them and told them that there was a way. Because of their special circumstances, God decided to have each of them serve as a mentor, teacher and protector over the captives that went on to become slaves on earth. They had to provide this service for two hundred years. The service is for the slaves and descendants of the slaves.

SPIRITUAL CONNECTION

As a part of this spiritual connection, Amadou, Ibrahima, Akim, Abdullah and Zumbulu had a charge to seek out and to console, guide, protect, and inspire slaves and their descendants. This responsibility manifested itself in many different ways. Often it could mean that they may have to follow a slave his entire lifetime. This could mean telling ideas to the slaves including thoughts of rebellion. It could also mean teaching tolerance and providing coping mechanisms in order to deal with less than human conditions the slave had to endure. This assignment could also be accomplished by connecting with the slaves' descendants in generations to come.

THE ASSIGNMENTS SPIRITUAL VINDICATION, AFTER THE ASSIGNMENT

The five spirits were earthward bound and found their subjects in the southeastern part of the United States. Over the next two hundred years, they would look for slaves and their descendants to work with.

Amadou in his past life was the son of a chieftain and a very skilled warrior. One of his most interesting assignments was a slave owned by a very cruel master. Amadou as a skilled warrior generally fought against overwhelming odds. The slave that Amadou bonded with was named Nat. Nat possessed the same characteristics as Amadou. This made this assignment very challenging. Amadou helped Nat by transmitting ideas and strategies of rebellion to his mind. He then nurtured these ideas until they became plans and thus a reality. Nat eventually became the most feared slave in the United States. He participated in and inspired uprisings in most southern states. Nat continued with this activity until he was caught and hanged.

Ibrahima on the other hand, was a learned scholar and teacher of the ways of Allah. In his past life he often settled disputes using logic and nonviolent techniques. He looked for those assignments that were best suited to use these principles. Ibrahima's most interesting subject was not a slave but was a descendent of slaves. Slavery was abolished, but the conditions for their descendants were very appalling.

His assignment was a very young and skilled communicator. He believed in equal treatment for all regardless of race. This young man was named Martin. Ibrahima would visit him as he meditated. He would share thoughts and the use of nonviolent techniques that proved to be very effective.

Akim was a farmer in his past life. Back in his African village he was responsible for teaching the young farmers how to get the most yields out of their crops. He also taught them how to rotate their crops and harvest food for the village. As a spirit, he traveled over much of the southern part of the United States. Most of the slaves brought to this country worked on small farms or large plantations. He bonded with many slaves by giving them ideas and communicating techniques that would make their work easier. His most interesting assignment was a farmer named George. George did extraordinary things with the peanut plant. As fast as Akim could share new ideas with him, He developed new products from this plant.

Abdullah was a fierce warrior in his past life. He was respected in his village and the neighboring villages in Africa. He could not be defeated by any single man in his territory. When his village was at war with one of the tribes of another region, he was singled out as the warrior that had to be stopped. The opposing king charged seven of his most skilled and disciplined soldiers to capture Abdullah. The king offered his men a very rich purse if this feat was accomplished. The men were successful and the king immediately sold him to the slave traders.

Abdullah as a spirit searched the United States for subjects to bond with.

He finally came across this giant of a man that reminded him of himself. This young man was a descendent of slaves. He was very proud of his body. Abdullah thought he would be a very promising prospect. Abdullah began to tell with this young man named Jack. He planted the idea in the man's mind to become a prize fighter. Abdullah shared ways the young man could condition his body and develop fighting strategies. This young man went on to become the first of his race to be a great prize fighter.

Zumbulu was a music maker in his native West African village. He did his musical shows to entertain the king and other dignitaries. His music served as background for many dance troupes. Neighboring tribes would visit to see the performances put on by the great Zumbulu.

As a mentor and teacher in the spirit world, Zumbulu followed many slaves that showed promise. Near the end of his two hundred years of service, he connected with a descendant of a slave that possessed tremendous talent. This individual was nicknamed The Duke by his peers. Zumbulu often entered the dreams of this young genius sharing themes and ideas for many compositions. This young man had an insatiable appetite for developing, arraigning and composing tune after tune. As fast as Zumbulu could enter his dreams with new ideas the music was flowing like water. The Duke was writing and arraigning music for many musicians. This subject gave Zumbulu the most satisfaction.

-PREFACE # 2-

A SUMMER TO REMEMBER

This is a story about a young boy named jack who grew up in Baltimore, Md. in the late 1940's and early 1950's. Jack had a special relationship with his maternal grandfather. His grandfather lived on a small farm in rural South Carolina. Jack used to spend some summers with his grandfather and enjoyed the peacefulness of country life. The story takes place on the farm during one of Jack's summer visits.

LIFE IN THE CITY

As a black youth growing up in the late 40's and early 50's, Jack was not aware of many problems his ancestors experienced. His life up to that time was confined to one or two blocks in West Baltimore. Everything he experienced was within those two blocks. There was one exception; however, school was three blocks away. The church he attended was across the street from his house. He had a part time job at the neighborhood barber shop. He earned a couple of dollars a week to keep it clean.

There were many families that lived on his block. Practically all of the families were renters. There were just a few homeowners on the entire block. Most of the houses were three stories with two apartments to a floor. Some apartments had to share bathrooms. Many people lived on this block Jack knew every family there. When Jack was eleven or twelve years old he started visiting his grandparents in South Carolina.

COUNTRY LIFE

Jack always looked forward to visiting his grandparents in the country. Things seemed so much better there. He did not have to deal with all the noise of the city. Country air was cleaner and so much easier to breathe. The entire environment was cleaner. There were not nearly as many restrictions in country life as there were in the city.

Jack especially enjoyed the relationship he had with his grandfather. He helped his grandfather work the farm. He spent quality time with him when he visited. His grandfather shared many stories about the farm and his ancestors. The visits to the country lasted from two weeks to an entire summer.

ONE SPECIAL SUMMER

One summer when Jack became thirteen years old his parents let him spend the entire summer with his grandfather. His grandmother had died recently and his grandfather looked forward to having Jack spend the summer. His grandfather began to share more stories of the difficulty black people had growing up in the south. Jack learned that his great grandfather was a slave on some of the same land where his grandfather now had his farm. The farm was a part of Rhodes' plantation. Slaves endured many hardships and cruel treatment.

When Jack finished his chores for the day, he had a favorite place he would go to relax. A little distance from the farmhouse was a large willow tree. Jack would sit under this tree and often fall asleep. A very interesting thing happened to Jack one evening after finishing his work around the farm. He fell asleep on his favorite spot under the willow tree. He woke up to the sounds of distress. Jack looked around the area and saw nothing unusual. He dozed off again and heard what he thought were sound of distress. Jack looked in the direction of the sound and heard the words barely audible. Mercy...! Mercy...! He saw a large poplar tree some ways from the willow tree. Again he heard the voice. Please do not treat me this way. This started to spook Jack. He thought about the stories his grandfather told him. He suddenly realized that this could be the voice of a spirit. His grandfather told him some awful things had happened to black people. Jack knew that his grandfather's farm was once a part of a large plantation that owned many slaves.

An hour had passed and Jack did not hear any more voices. He went back to the farmhouse and told his grandfather what he had experienced. He tried to just brush it off as a dream because he did not want his grandfather to worry. Jack's grandfather was bothered by what he heard. He felt responsible because he had shared so many stories with Jack. His grandfather suggested to him that maybe he should find another favorite place he could retreat too. The grandfather sensed that this was bothering Jack and he was careful not to share any more stories.

THE ENCOUNTER

A week had passed and Jack avoided going near his old willow tree. He searched the farm for another quiet place but none measured up to the spot under the tree. There was just no other place that could satisfy Jack. Jack would automatically be walking toward the tree when he would catch himself and turn away. It was as if he were being drawn to the willow tree like it was a magnet. He tried very hard not to go toward the tree but found himself pulled in that direction.

One day Jack decided to put his fears behind him and asked God to protect him from any evil that may be lurking around the tree. Jack walked directly to his favorite spot. He sat under the tree for thirty minutes and felt calmness come over him. Calmness gave way to sleep, which he tried to avoid. Jack quickly woke up, but remained very peaceful and quiet. While awake he thought he heard a sound. There! He heard it again. A voice called out. "Please help me." Jack's first reaction was to run. He stayed to face whatever unknown force was out there. He was relying on his faith in God to protect him. In front of the poplar tree, Jack saw a blurred image of a man appear. Jack walked very slowly toward this figure. Again, Jack heard the voice. "Please help me." Jack saw what was the image of a black man in chains and torn clothes. How can I help you? The voice from the image asked,

"Have you seen my Enzenga?" Who is Enzenga?" asked Jack, and" Who are you"? " I am Akim." Enzenga was my beautiful young bride.

We were captured in Africa and sold to traders. Jack asked,"How did you get here?" We were held in a place called" Ballmor, Merlin." There was a slave pen named Donovan's slave Pen. I was separated from my Enzenga when I was sold to a man representing Rhodes' plantation in South Carolina. Enzenga was sold to a plantation owner in Georgia. This happened from the Frederick Street dock in" Ballmor, Merlin." You mean Baltimore, Maryland. That's where I am from." I gots to find my Enzenga" replied the spirit. "How come you so messed up"? Asked Jack. I heard my master talking to a slave master from Georgia. He was bragging about this beautiful black wench he had purchased. He said he had named her Susie Mae. She told him her name was Enzenga and she was married to a prince named Akim. He then laughed and told her, She be his wench now. That slave master from Georgia told my Enzenga that her name was Susie Mae and he did not want to hear no more talk of no Enzenga. He also told her that she would be his wench and would sleep in the big house with him and his miss Ann. That slave master let out a big laugh and kept on laughing." I knew that be my Enzenga he talking bout". I know I had to find her. That is when I started to run. I just had to find her. I run, two three times and get caught. Old masser had me tied to post and whip me till I bleed. He then pours salt in my wounds. I be still thinking bout Enzenga and soon as I get my strength back I run again. This time old masser say he make a xzamble out of me and he gawna stop my running for good. Well, masser tied me to this poplar tree and whipped my body raw. Next thing I know he be pouring oil all over my body. Last thing I member, I be smelling smoke and feel my flesh burning. I still be looking for my Enzenga.

Jack finally replied, "Well, you know you are dead, don't you. You are now a ghost. Do you know what year this is? Hey spirit, the year is now 1955. What year did all this happen to you? The spirit replied," It happened in 1843. That is over one hundred years ago. Your Enzenga is probably dead too. The spirit was very quiet. Jack also informed the spirit that this part of Rhodes' plantation is now his grandfather's farm. "No fooling," said the spirit. There was also a great Civil War in this country and slavery was abolished in 1865. "No fooling." Jack informed the spirit it was now time for him to rest and he need to ask almighty God to grant him his peace. Then clouds formed and it began to rain. It rained for a short time and then the sun shone very bright. Jack asked the spirit to follow the light. The spirit vanished and peace and tranquility again came over the land. Jack returned to his place under the old willow tree to ponder his experience.

A short time later Jack went back to the old farmhouse to talk to his grandfather. He told him everything that happened down by the old willow tree. Jack's grandfather listened to him very intensely. When Jack finished, his grandfather told him of a story passed down by his father. It was about a slave who called himself Akim that was constantly running away. This slave was put to death in the manner that Jack had explained to him. Jack's grandfather never told him this story because he did not want to frighten the boy. From that time forward, Jack never heard any more voices when he stopped by the old willow tree.

Andrew Lunn Sr.

Andrew Lunn Sr.

ABOUT THE AUTHOR:

INSPIRATION FOR POEMS:

The author has provided thirty years of service to the Baltimore community in the area of health and human services. Six years in the anti-poverty program and twenty four years in the Baltimore City Health Department This experience exposed him to real life struggles of residents in various communities and their ability to cope with a society in transition.

He was born in Baltimore, Md. The seventh of ten children. He is a product of the Baltimore City Public School system and a graduate of Morgan State University. The author has compiled a variety of topics and subject matter using a sensitive and human approach. This is evidenced by his poems and short stories. The material for this book is based on personal experiences, historical events and contemporary issues. The poems will stir emotions, motivate, captivate and inspire the audience.

The first poem written by the author "Tribute to Big Brother" reflects the life of the author's oldest brother who departed this life on Mother's Day in 1996. It is about the love and impact the oldest brother had on family members and the many lives he touched while doing God's work as a minister.

Other poems the author considers love poems are "The Day I Saw An Angel" and "Memories Of Love".

These poems were written in memory of and a tribute to the author's first wife who died of Cancer in 1984 two days before Christmas. They do not dwell on the sickness but the love they shared with each other and the many lives that were touched by such an incredible individual.

The poems "Mother" and " Black Woman" represents the author's memory of his own mother as he was growing up and the struggles the black woman has had down through history in providing for and keeping her family together. Many of the attributes are obviously characteristics of mothers everywhere regardless of their ethnicity.

"Legacy of Love" is a poem written for a tree planting ceremony by the author to express the family's love and devotion for their mother. She was fondly called "Moah" by her children and grand children alike.

Many stories have been told of the plight of African Slaves and their journey from their homeland and arrival to the shores of the Americas. "Journey into Hell" is an attempt by the author to visualize what it must have been like to be a part of such an experience. The poems "Blues A Black Perspective", Lynching and "Under the Willow Tree describes what life was like for a black man in America after experiencing the ordeal of slavery. "Under the Willow Tree" was a poem that the author was inspired to write by stories shared with him by his maternal grandfather who grew up in the rural south over a century ago.

The poems "Anger", "Enemy in the Village" and "Violence" deals with some of the problems facing our community and the authors attempt to inspire the readers to look for alternative methods of solving and coping with these issues. The author's lengthy service to the community exposed him to many of the experiences he outlines in these poems. He often reflects back to a time when the entire community was an extended family.

The American system of justice has not always dealt fairly with the Black Man . In some cases it has contributed to the negative images of black people in this country. The news media has also contributed to the negative images by focusing on the bad things and not showing enough positive things in our community. The following poems were written to inspire black youth not to get caught in the criminal justice system but focus on getting a good education, and to take responsibility for themselves and their young families. Poems like "Hostile Environment", "Conspiracy", "Cry Baby" and"Fathers in the Hood" were meant to inform, educate and motivate the youth to achieve new heights and not fall victim to the many obstacles that are in their paths on the road to success.

The author wrote a number of poems based on the black experience from his perspective. He shares what it was like growing up during segregation and the positive and negative impact it had on his life. The poem " Pennsylvania Avenue, The Glory Days" describes the avenue as the showcase of the black community. It was a time when black business thrived during segregation. Well known musicians and entertainers frequented the avenue and could be enjoyed by the majority of black citizens for a nominal fee. This poem was written to inform the youth of the proud history of Pennsylvania Avenue in Baltimore City and the role black people played in making it great.

On the other hand,"Black Man" and "Who AM I" share the struggles of Blacks to get a voice and to be recognized for their contributions in our society. Not only to be called on in the time of need, but to share equitably in the Nation's prosperity."Black Man" also outlines many of the positive contributions made by blacks but how easily it can be negated by the negative actions of a few of its youth.

"Ancestral Spirit Connection" was written by the author to express his feeling of being connected to and having a kinship to the African continent. This connection comes in the form of a spirit making contact as a nubian warrior who is a guardian angel over blacks in this land. The spirit is impressed by the achievements of blacks seen as lost children who needs to be protected and made knowledgeable about their heritage.

"My Love Of Music" was written by the author to express his love of music. This poem has been recited and read by the author at open mike poetry readings. Once interviewed by aa producer for Maryland Public Television the author said of this poem that he could not sing, play a musical instrument or write music.

His love of music comes in the written word by way of his poem.

Other poems included in the book express the author's feelings on various subjects. On the lighter side some will make you laugh. One such poem that is often requested at his readings is" Fish Sandwich and A Bottle Of Beer". This poem grew out of an experience that the author had while visiting relatives at a family reunion in a small southern town many years ago. Much of the story has been exaggerated to add a little flavor but proves to be very amusing.

The poem "False Hope" grew out of an experience the author had while visiting a casino on a fun trip. He saw so many interesting things and strange behaviors that he decided to write about his experiences. He found himself exhibiting many of the same attitudes and behaviors he noticed in others.

The author was inspired to write the poem "Loss Treasures" based on his experience with the public school system which gave him an opportunity to observe students, teachers and parents. This poem captures some of that experience in dramatic fashion and offers hope of how we can correct some of the ills.

"Caribbean Woman" and "My First Carnival in T&T" are poems reflecting the author's relationship and experiences in the Caribbean and experiencing the culture through his wife who is from Trinidad. The author has visited many Caribbean islands but never really had an appreciation for the culture until he met his wife, who exposed him to carnival in T&T.

The author naturally being a music lover adopted soca and calypso right behind his first love which is jazz. Being a part of the carnival experience has broadened his knowledge and understanding of the people from the Caribbean. His wife and her family and friends has played an integral part in this transformation. "My First Carnival In T&T" is a rather lengthy poem which explains most of the dynamics of carnival as seen and experienced through the eyes of a foreigner. It allows the audience to travel along with the author and experience through his eyes the beauty and excitement of carnival in T&T. A " Trini " National on the other hand would read this poem and get homesick. The author's outgoing personality and his willingness to accept people made his new experience easy. After many years of seeing and participating in carnival in T&T, the author gets homesick like so many other" Trinis "just from the mention of the word carnival.

America has often been referred to as a melting pot. A blend of different races and
ethnic groups which contributes to its greatness. The author expresses the strengths and some concerns in his poem"The Melting Pot".

"Terrorism in America" is a poem the author was inspired to write after that dreadful experience on September 11, 2001. It is certain to stir the emotions and raise your level of patriotism.

The author shares two short stories that evolved from two poems in this collection. The first is "From the Depths Of The Middle Passage" which is a spin off of "Journey into Hell". It is a story of the plight of African Slaves making the journey from Africa to America but never making it through the middle passage.

The second story is developed from the poem "Under the Willow Tree" It is a story about a young boy named Jack that grew up in the city but had a special relationship with his grandfather in rural South Carolina. The story is "A Summer To Remember".

www.ingramcontent.com/pod-product-compliance
Lightning Source LLC
Chambersburg PA
CBHW030357290526
45785CB00004B/1794